A gift for:

From:

Edited by Helen Exley
Illustrations by Juliette Clarke
Words by Pam Brown

Published in 2012 and 2021 by Helen Exley® LONDON in Great Britain.
All the words by Pam Brown © Helen Exley Creative Ltd 2012, 2021.
Illustrated by Juliette Clarke © Helen Exley Creative Ltd 2012, 2021.
Design, selection and arrangement © Helen Exley Creative Ltd 2012, 2021.

ISBN 978-1-78485-320-4

12 11 10 9 8 7 6 5 4 3 2 1

OTHER HELEN EXLEY GIFTBOOKS:

For my Mother 365	Friendship 365	Happy Days! 365
The Secrets of Happiness 365	Inspiration 365	Yes to life! 365
365 Days with my bossy Cat	For my Sister 365	Calm Days 365

Helen Exley® LONDON, 16 Chalk Hill, Watford, Herts WD19 4BG, UK
www.helenexley.com

January 1

My Daughter, totally yourself.
Bright as a button and eager for the world.

If you love this giftbook…

… you will probably want to know how to find other HELEN EXLEY®
gifts like it. They're all listed on

www.helenexley.com

Helen Exley and her team have specialised in finding wonderful quotations
for gifts on wisdom, calm and between families, friends, lovers…
A major part of Helen's work has been to bring love and communication within
families by finding and publishing the things people everywhere would like to say
to the people they love.

Her books obviously strike a chord because they now appear in forty-five languages,
and are distributed in more than eighty countries.

You can follow us on and

MIX
Paper from
responsible sources
FSC® C081635

How could I ever have anticipated
the joy you have given me?

December 31

We remember all the days that are gone,
and the joy you have given us
– and we look forward to the joy to come.
Bless you always.

January 3

Surprises. Amazement.
She is your
diamond daughter.
She can cut across
your heart and mind.

December 30

Gather up your courage,
your talents and your dreams. Be determined.
Face your fears. Cling on to hope. And if you fail,
get up and go on running.
I wish you joy – In love. In life.

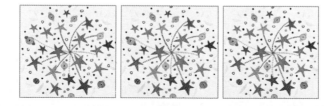

January 4

In you my life begins again.

December 29

My *Wishes For You*
The true joy of love is only shaped by time.
I wish you that discovery, that happiness.

Like it or not,
we are bound to one another.
It is the lightest of links –
so light that sometimes
we seem to forget it altogether.
But it is stronger
than life itself.

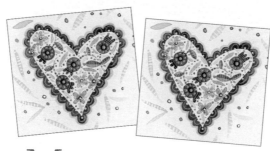

May you know friendship.
May you know love.

January 6

A LOVING DAUGHTER IS
THE MOST PRECIOUS OF GIFTS.

Whatever happens...our lives are stitched together by a thread of gold that cannot change, whatever changes come.

All parents worry
about all daughters
at all times.
The best cure is to hear
them laughing.

December 26

Whenever you meet beauty,
we are beside you. You can never be lonely
– for our love is always with you.

January 8

A Very, Very Special Daughter

Happiness beyond anything you ever thought possible.

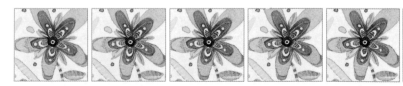

December 25

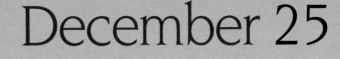

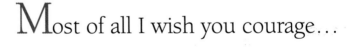
Most of all I wish you courage…

Little daughter...
She is so beautiful,
so funny, so eager,
so resolute.
And she loves you
with all her heart.

December 24

If I could give you anything
it would be a quietness
at the very heart of your life
that would remain
tranquil and certain
whatever befell.

Having a daughter is like being involved
in a perpetual treasure hunt – surprises at every turn!

You have to fight your own battles, love.
But I'm here in your corner with the bucket
and sponge.

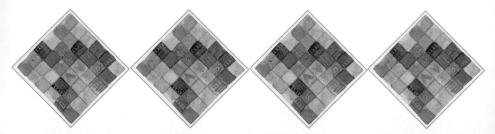

Small daughters give you
hugs and sticky kisses
and cry if they are scolded,
and climb into your bed
when they are frightened,
and give you presents…
And teach you how to love.

December 22

It's good when a mother and her daughter
store things in their minds to tell each other.
People they've met,
things they've done, delights...
Small threads that bind them together
in love and understanding.

How small my world
until you came along.

December 21

When all the world is dreary,
I think about my daughter,
her brightness and her laughter,
and life comes right again.

You dance for me, sing for me,
travel the world for me.

How clever you are.
How beautiful.
How kind.
But, best of all
how loving.

January 14

Your daughter grows
and there are unhoped-for gifts –
successes, wisdom, new discoveries.
Friendship. Laughter.

December 19

You are a kaleidoscope.
Constantly changing. Always new.
The patterns shift but always fascinate.
Beautiful. Strange. Bewildering.
But always you.

January 15

When no one else understands,
A daughter does.

December 18

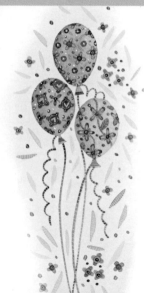

I am continually amazed by you – my lovely, unpredictable daughter.

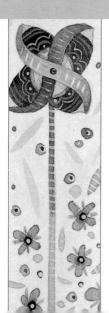

Thank you for
bringing exclamation marks
to our existence.

December 17

Thank you for all the prezzies – serious and silly.
Scent and stockings, rose bushes, kumquats,
tea and chocolate mice. Fine paintings.
Ginger and liquorice. Garlic and poppadoms.
Yo-yos and teddy bears.

Keep a little
of this innocence,
this clear, untarnished joy,
this trust,
this eagerness,
whatever comes.

December 16

Thank you for all the years
you've given us. Years to treasure.
Our dearest daughter.
Our lovely lass.

January 18

Where are you going, my girl?
I cannot guess –
Only hope that it will all
be wonderful.
All I can promise is that I will do
all I can do to make it so.

December 15

Dearest daughter. One tiny tug will have me dropping anything I'm engaged in – you are, above everything, the heartbeat of my life.

January 19

Looking back to the day you were born
we smile. How could we begin to suspect
the astonishments
held in the bundle of blanket?

December 14

...And all of it has combined
to make you what you are.
Our special daughter.
Our loving –
and most dearly loved lass.

Heads of petunias.
Fluff-covered toffees.
A lifetime of gifts.
A lifetime of loving.
But best of all,
dearest, is knowing
you're mine.

December 13

Thank you for your vast determination.
Your mastering of skills.
Your trust. Your welcoming.
Your love.

January 21

A thank-you to my daughter
For seeing to it that my life is never dull,
for keeping me on my toes.

December 12

Dear Daughter
Live a most happy life
– your own.
Unique and brave
and wonderful.

January 22

BRAVE, KIND, LOVING
– THAT'S MY GIRL.
SPECIAL.
WONDERFUL.

December 11

How could I ever have produced
someone so clever, so kind, so loving,
so special as you?
But how very glad I am that I did.

Daughters –
keep us going
well after
our sell-by date.

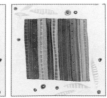

December 10

You are there for me
– however far away you are.
We share our highs and lows.
You are your own assured
and independent self –
yet still a part of me.
Dear lass. Dear daughter.

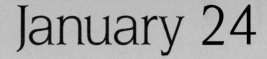

January 24

We have a daughter,
and are baffled from the very first,
as she grows and changes
by the minute. Utterly herself.
Most dear of all possessions
– yet never totally possessed.

You have my love –
the love that links us.
Take it with you into the world
that I will never know.

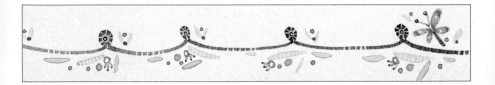

January 25

Daughter
Every single day
you astonish
or delight me
— and often both.

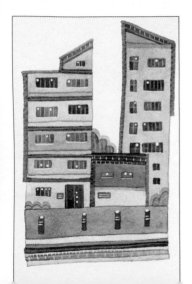

Go where I never dared to go.
Live a life worth living.

January 26

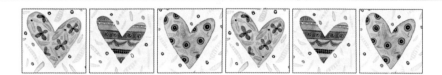

Loved you the second I saw you.
Love you all the more with each passing year.

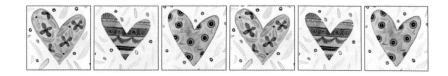

You can never be lonely
– for our love is always with you.

A daughter's good news
brightens my drabbest day.

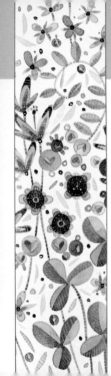

December 6

Even the worst of times
are balanced out by those of joy,
success, sharing and laughter.
Days to remember
with a happy heart.

January 28

Thank you for wilting dandelions,
for twigs of blossom,
for wet pebbles,
for fluff-covered toffees,
for sticky kisses.
Thank you for loving me.

My dearest girl –
source of silly surprises,
unexpected hugs,
laughter, comfort.

January 29

Do it all, my love!
Fly. Swim. Sail.
Climb. Dance. Sing.
You've only one lifetime.
Start *now* if you want
to fit it all in.

December 4

I wish you success
that has no sting.
I wish you joy and peace and warm
contentment.
And always, always, love.

Dearest Daughter.
I wish you happy.
Now and always.

December 3

Life has been very kind to me.
It has given me you.

January 31

To have a daughter to us
it is a miracle. Greatest of gifts.
Dearest of daughters.

December 2

Your daughter may not become or do
the things you dreamed of.
She may not become a doctor,
a prima ballerina, an archaeologist,
a lawyer. She may not marry.
She may not have children.
But what does it matter? She is herself.
Unique. Valuable. Your own.

February 1

Thank you for all the unexpected phone calls,
the envelopes stuffed with cuttings and drawings
and dried leaves and photographs – and letters
apparently written while riding a camel!

December 1

I'm proud of all
your achievements.
But I'm most proud of
your being just you.
You are special to me
whatever you do.

February 2

Thank you for your
wonder at the world.

A parent and child have a relationship different to any other – whatever loves, whatever hates, lie between them, they are bound together.

There comes a day
when a daughter
becomes a friend.

However much we disagree
I need your life to interlock with mine,
to know you share my secrets and my joys.
To know that you are there.

A small daughter looks at her mother
and promises herself she will never act
like that or speak like that or make such
daft mistakes. But she will. She will.

November 28

Thank you, dearest, for all the Birthday and Mother's Day Suprizzles. But thank you most of all for the Un-Birthday remembrances.

February 5

A daughter reminds
you of all the things
you had forgotten
about being young.

November 27

What a lot of fuss we make over disappointments
and failures and the loss of material things.
When all that really matters is that the family
have each other – and you.

February 6

I wish you joy
– success and friendship.
Love.
Wonder and discovery.

I wish for you courage
and clear thinking,
hope and a happy heart.
Always.

Clear eyes, unblemished skin,
and hair as soft as thistledown.
A laugh that is all delight.
A smile, all love.
Your rounded arms stretched
out to me. Your head nestled
in my shoulder.

Mothers and fathers never
cease to be astonished by their daughters.

February 8

There you are, taller than I am,
more streetwise than I am –
and gentle too.
Kind. Loving. More complex
than I ever dreamed.
And happy. I am proud of you.

Thank you for the little things
    – a pat in passing
    – a snuggle, a hug
– a friendly wink, a smile.
A cup of tea.
Buttered toast.
A rose in a milk bottle.
The little things that make
    my life possible.

Before a daughter
has finally decided who she is
and what she wants to be,
her family are near bankrupt.
Ice skates. Flute. Ballet shoes.
Riding breeches. Paints.
Theatrical make-up. Scuba gear.
Microscope.

November 23

Little things outlast great triumphs.
Here is the ghost of little fingers clasping
your hand, here are arms stretched out to greet you;
here is a face uplifted for your kiss. The child has grown
and gone away – and yet the sweetness stays.

What do I most wish for you?
A belief in the fundamental
worth of humankind, and that,
my dear, includes yourself.

November 22

Love, courage and an enquiring mind.
That's what I wish for you.
Together with the ability to stand
in other people's shoes.
And to laugh at yourself.

February 11

You lighten my days
and lift my spirits.
In you I am young again.

November 21

When you were very small
you made me plasticine pots
and pictures of myself
– all hair and smile and skinny legs.
Caterpillars and stones.
Fluffy toffees. Poems.
I have them still. Safe and protected.

February 12

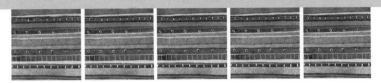

Daughters rarely do the things you dread.
They choose the things you never bargained for.

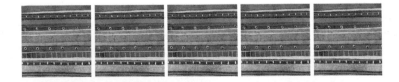

November 20

As you grew
and smiled and began
to speak
every day brought
a new delight.

February 13

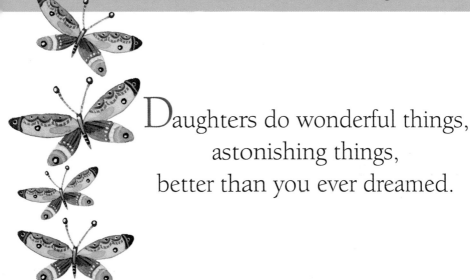

Daughters do wonderful things,
astonishing things,
better than you ever dreamed.

November 19

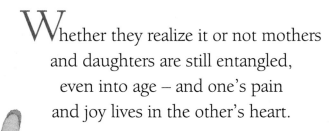

Whether they realize it or not mothers
and daughters are still entangled,
even into age – and one's pain
and joy lives in the other's heart.

Here you are, my lovely daughter.
Safe and sound.
Welcome and wonderful.
In no way like anyone else.

Daughters never quite forgive you
for throwing out the clothes you wore at twenty.
Apparently they're In.

You change and you grow
– but are forever
my dearest daughter.

A daughter and her mother are so entwined in heart and mind that, gladly or unwillingly, they share each love, each joy, each sorrow and each bitter wrong lifelong.

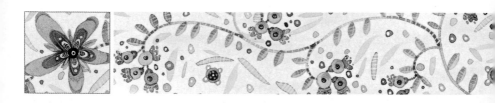

We are so proud of all you have become.

However sad I am, a note or a text
from you brings me happiness.

February 17

Dear Daughter. I hope that when you are very, very old you can look back and say "Heavens. That was a lovely life."

Now we meet as equals,
having forgiven one another,
having learned to love,
having rediscovered laughter.

A daughter's clothes
can be very silly indeed.
As silly as yours were at the same age.
Just differently silly.

A father looks forward
to the time when he has a daughter
– and can make and build
with the most amazing care –
her very own castle!

February 19

How angry you were to be born.
How you flailed your arms and bawled
till you were crimson.
How you wished you'd
stayed all snug and undisturbed.
But I held you close and showed you
sunlight, leaf shadows, yellow daisies –
and you smiled and began
to discover wonder.

November 13

Each day has been a wonder
and astonishment.

Thank you for seeing to it
that my life never gets monotonous.
Extraordinary decisions.
Extraordinary adventures.
Et voila!!

November 12

Thank you for your vast determination.
Your triumphs over gravity. Your mastering
of skills. Your trust. Your welcoming.
Your love.

February 21

Dear Daughter – eight months old,
all smiles and happy jabberwock,
most loving, most fascinated by the world.
This was the best time. But, then.
So was the day of your birth,
the day you recognised me,
the day you first sat up.
Each day has been the best.

November 11

Even in a non-kissy,
non-cuddly family
invisible cuddles and kisses
wrap you round.

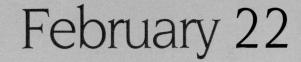

February 22

Memories have linked our lives
so often and so long
that we are almost one.
I am myself – and you are totally unique.
Yet we are linked forever.
By experience. By love.

November 10

Your mind is amazed at all the wonders of the world.
Grow, my dear daughter, learn and love.

February 23

How fast time spins another generation
– child giving way to child – joy to joy.

How strange, how wonderful
to find one's daughter understands things
beyond one's comprehension.
Higher mathematics. Greek.
Physics or Cordon Bleu.
How to mend a fuse.
Or ride a motor bike.

February 24

Thank you for the train rides
and the roller-coasters.
Thank you for running with me
in the rain. And sprawling with me
in the summer sun.

November 8

So little time ago you ran to me,
small arms spread wide
and love and laughter in your face.
But Time is kind.
It simply changes joy.
I hear your knock
and see your smile
and am young again.

February 25

Each day brings new surprises,
new delights.
And with them anxieties...
never known before.

Our girl. You are grown long since,
but still I remember the weight of you
across my shoulders, the clasp of your hands
about my neck, your laughter in my ears.

February 26

When you were small we tried
to stand between you and sorrow.
And now, when we are old,
you have taken on that role
and with loving hearts
fend off the years and
take the weight of our anxieties.

The world is yours.
Fly free.

A daughter may want
to follow in your footsteps.
Or climb Everest.

Daughters are like a very complex recipe. You start off with confidence and hope – then reach a stage of such difficulty that you feel it has all gone horribly and irretrievably wrong. But, at last, you find to your astonishment and delight a totally unexpected transformation. She's come out perfect!

February 28/29

Thank you for believing
my birthday cakes were magical,
my paintings amazing, my stories
the best in the world…

November 4

I wish you happy and secure
and comfortable and wise. But not yet.
Get the adventures in first.

March 1

I worry about you.
Whether you're happy or sad.
If you have succeeded.
If you have failed.
…Near or far away,
that's what mothers do.

November 3

Thank you for showing me,
when I thought my mothering days
were over, that the best days
between us are only just beginning.

I live two lives.
Mine and yours.

May you find all
the good things you deserve.
My dear daughter.

Everything comes in useful in the end.
All the mistakes, all the pain, all the loss
– just as much as the hard work and the learning
and the love.

November 1

I could have been rich.
I could have been famous
but these things are very doubtful.
I had you and that was a sure
and certain victory.

Your daughter.
Your joy and your anxiety forever.

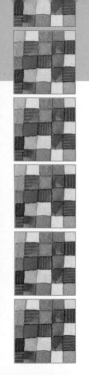

October 31

I loved you as a baby,
plump as a piglet,
as a school child,
awkward and eager,
as a teenager, totally confused.
And now most of all
wise and funny and adventurous
– my dearest friend.

When you were little
you gave me forget-me-nots and daisies.
Now you give me
a world of wonder.

Love encompasses everything
– dark and dull and shining gold. She's yours,
and you're hers. Forever.

Light the blue touch-paper
and stand well back.
She may be a squib or a rocket.
But wonderful!

Every year you grow
more dear to me.

Dad has long and earnest conversations with his baby daughter. He tells her she is noisy, undisciplined and manipulative – and she will be sent back if she doesn't pull herself together. And the baby smiles complacently. She has him exactly where she wants him.

Thanks for all the cards
– hand drawn or by Renoir
...for all the parcels – knobbly
or beribboned.

March 8

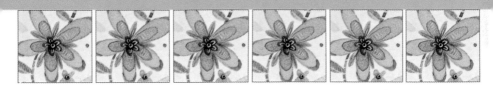

The happiest of wishes to our most
astonishing delightful daughter…
And thank you for the years of wonder
that made you what you are.

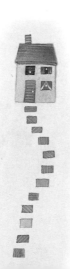

We know your strength
But – never forget!
In case of dire emergency
We're here!

No daughter decides to give up any hobby
until her parents have bought all the required kit.

October 26

I am so very ordinary.
How then did I produce a girl like you?
So beautiful,
so clever and so kind.

March 10

Wherever you are –
in city street or in the hush
and glimmer of
a summer wood –
our love is with you.
It shines in the quiet pool.
It wheels above you
in the flight of geese.

October 25

May you always find
something to delight you.

The older you get,
the dearer you become.

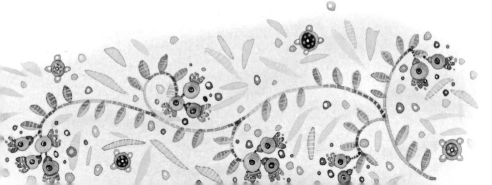

October 24

There are only a few things
I couldn't do without.
And you're one of them.

March 12

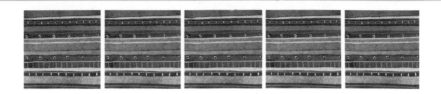

Just when you've settled to worrying
about your teenage daughter,
you suddenly realise the teenage years
are passed – and she's fine!

October 23

I am so proud of you.
Proud of your courage and your concern
for others, your resilience, your love of life.
Proud of all that you've achieved.
Your creativity. Your willingness to learn
– so much in one small person!

March 13

Your first swan. Your first day by the sea.
Your first walk through a field of spring flowers.
The first time you heard and loved Mozart.
In sharing your childhood discoveries,
I have relived my own.

We exasperate one another
but that is half the fun.
We are part of one another
forever and forever.

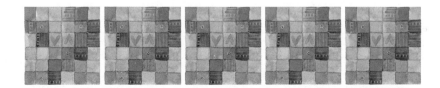

March 14

You were a very lovely baby
– but you've improved with every passing year.

October 21

A parent holds her like a flower,
like thinnest glass.
We wonder at this new and lovely life,
incredible in its perfection.
We grow with her, learning as we go.

Mothers worry about their babies,
their toddlers, their teenagers
and do their best
to keep them safe and happy.
Even when they are grandmas.
They can't help it.

A daughter always
has something new
with which
to astonish you.

March 16

Here's your writing on an envelope
and the day is no longer dull.

October 19

A daughter – a gift to the world.

March 17

Thank you for all the gifts.
The lukewarm tea.
The poems and the paintings. The plants.
The flowerings of your heart
and mind. A little of yourself.

A daughter never ceases
to spring surprises.

March 18

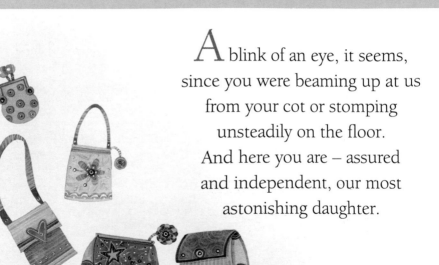

A blink of an eye, it seems,
since you were beaming up at us
from your cot or stomping
unsteadily on the floor.
And here you are – assured
and independent, our most
astonishing daughter.

A daughter is a new beginning.

March 19

A daughter
makes life worthwhile.

Daughters can be erratic
in their correspondence
– but when you need them
they are there.

March 20

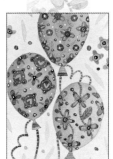

You see to it that
I am never, never bored.

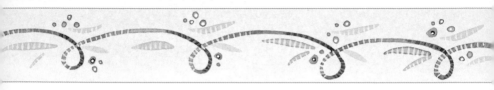

No one told you that you would feel
in your own heart every pain, every loss,
every disappointment, every rebuff, every cruelty
that your daughter experiences – life long.

March 21

Thank you for those years
of enchantment when you were very little –
the rapturous, toothless smiles,
the small perfections of your hands.

Any mother or father hits new lows
but "Luff you" sets all right.

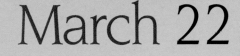

March 22

The best thing you have
given me is your friendship.

I always knew you were wonderful
– but you get better every day.

March 23

I wish you all good things
– especially the gift
of being able to let go.
Learn from sorrow
and mistakes. Then go on.

October 12

It is good to share the world
with a dear daughter.

March 24

I have done little with my life,
created nothing wonderful,
given no new knowledge to the world.
But I am content.
I have given it a daughter.
Most wonderful.
Most wise.

October 11

Thank you for all
the little astonishments
– a tuft of daisies,
a small lopsided pot,
a painting of us all.
A furry toffee.
A hug when I've been sad.
A song.

A small child sits in the middle of the table
and spreads her arms.
And in that gesture gathers us to her heart.
Her people, her loves, her world.

Like most parents I grow
despondent, thinking of the things
that I could never give you.
But then I remember.
I gave you life and, in consequence,
spring days of sun and rain,
the slap of water under
a dinghy's prow, waterfalls and
the high crags.

March 26

My daughter, my joy.
From the moment
I first saw you my life changed –
and at times, I'll admit,
I thought it for the worse!
But how dull,
how predictable life would
have been without you.

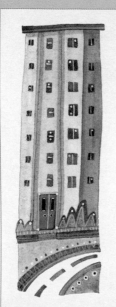

A daughter can lead you
into a wider world.

A daughter's triumph
is a parent's triumph.

A daughter is your
part in forever.

Every baby girl is utterly unique
and gives a special sort of love.

I love you now. This moment. As you are.
And I love you still – as when I first held you in my arms.
When you first took a step towards me.
When you first went to school
– and never looked back to wave. All those years
that make the lass I love – my dear, my precious girl.

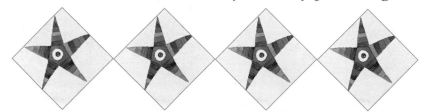

It's us against the world!
We argue, disagree
– and yet when the trouble
comes we are together.
Family!

Thank you
for reawakening wonder.

Parents try not to boast
too blatantly about their daughter.
But they can't help it.

October 5

I share your joys and successes –
but never forget I'm here for you when
things go wrong.

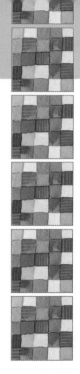

Daughters are liable
to opt for wearing rags – or worse.
To drop bombshells.
They are trying lives on for size.
The daughter you know and love
is still there.

Daughters are a delight.
Some of the time.
Most of the time.
When, that is, they are not
putting their white ballet tights
into the wash
inside black jeans! Daughters!

Daughters move away.
To study, to travel, to marry.
A thousand reasons.
And yet they never leave
– for they are a part of their
families forever.

You think you know your daughter
– and then she astonishes you.
Constantly.

April 2

To see one's daughter happy
is happiness enough.

October 2

Maybe I haven't done
the things I meant to.
But I had you.
And that is enough.
More, far more, than enough.

Thank you for those mornings
– just you and me in our dressing gowns,
tea and toast and talk.

October 1

Daughters are always astonished to discover
that their mother too was once young.
A little daft. A little confused.
A little awkward.
Argumentative, vulnerable,
given to falling flat on her face.
And so able to understand.

She appears not to listen to a word you say
– but in a few years
she'll be quoting you to her children
as the font of wisdom.

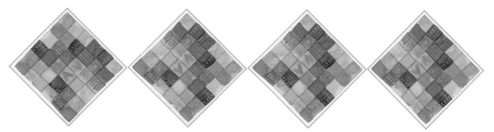

No one deserves to be loved as a daughter
loves – it is the world's wonder.

A daughter's smile
delights the heart.

September 29

Dear Daughter – you have shown yourself to be wise and good and kindly and loving. As in our hearts we always knew you would.

I know you. I know your courage
and good sense. I know that you will
build a good and happy life.
For yourself – and all about you.

September 28

There are daughters who give you lumpy parcels tied with string and there are daughters who give you gift-wrapped boxes elegant with flowers and bows and curly ribbons, but the contents are the same – affection under various guises.

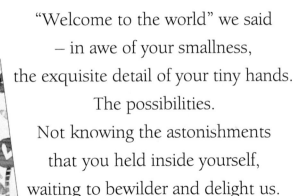

"Welcome to the world" we said
— in awe of your smallness,
the exquisite detail of your tiny hands.
The possibilities.
Not knowing the astonishments
that you held inside yourself,
waiting to bewilder and delight us.

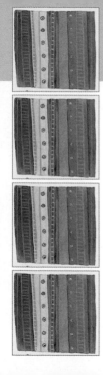

September 27

Daughters are daft. It's expected in
their teens, but they don't improve with age.
Walk out of university. Climb Everest.
Marry impossible men.
Their lives are rarely dull.
Just constant sources of anxiety.

Daughters are more precious than gold.
More precious than any inanimate thing,
however beautiful.

Thank you for giving me back young eyes and a young heart.

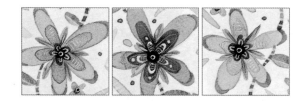

April 9

The day a mother
finds the perfect, right size,
almost new pair of boots
in the sales –
is the day her daughter
decides to give up
roller-skating.

September 25

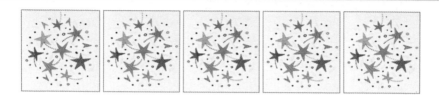

A daughter can be guaranteed
to do the unexpected,
it's what keeps life interesting.

Ride with me, straight and
beautiful; ride beside me.
Behind us lies the gentle country,
the patches where you stumbled.
Before us lies land stretching
to a wide horizon – your world
to discover and explore.

September 24

Daughters are like those small,
attractive, unnamed seedlings
that stun you by their sudden growth,
and explosion
into unexpected flower.

April 11

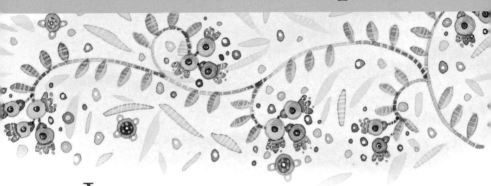

I wish you joy in the great things of life
– but also in the little things.
A flower, a bird, the friendship of a cat.

September 23

How fortunate I am to have a daughter like you. Someone to laugh with, share secrets, a reassurance in the darkest times. I look back on the happy times we've known – and wish you a year, a future, packed with delights.

Dear Daughter

Be a wife, a nun, an engine driver, a nurse,
an architect, a lady in a shoe shop.
Be what you want to be. What you need to be.
I'll back you all the way.

Legacy

Here, I am, counting the cost. All that I've gained.
Days of adventure. Days of despair. Down in the depths,
up in the air. All my confusion suddenly clear – my gift
to the future. My daughter. My dear.

We feel with her – each restlessness, each fear, each pain. She laughs and we are overjoyed.

September 21

A baby lies snug in its nutshell,
so small, so delicate, so vulnerable.
We feel inadequate to keep her safe,
to see her through to womanhood.
Not recognising the hidden strength
that will set her growing,
inch by inch, into a flowering tree.

A daughter is your excuse for playing with dolls again.

September 20

You came
and flung open
a window
to a wider world.

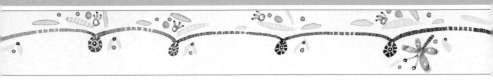

Mothers do a lot of worrying
about their daughters
– however capable and sensible they are.
It goes with the territory.

The jewel in my crown.
My own dear girl.

Thank you, my dearest girl, for emails,
gifts and letters that are exactly right.
Thank you for giving me advice. Thank you
for letting me into your life.

September 18

It's hard to accept that this tall, slender, beauty dressed entirely in a navy suit is the little girl who loved a frilly dress that swirled. And only a handful of years ago. But she's still crazy about peanut brittle!

Daughters can break
your heart and mend it.
Almost simultaneously.

September 17

How on earth did I produce so beautiful,
so caring, so capable, so kind, so gifted a daughter?
Thank you for coming into my life.

We've learned over years
patience and understanding,
loss and forgiveness.

Thank you for giving me something to boast about!

Daughters,
in their hour of triumph,
catch your eye and grin.

September 15

There are things I cannot stick together,
or heal with a hug... I wish I had some magic
that could make such things come right.
All I can do is be here. Always.

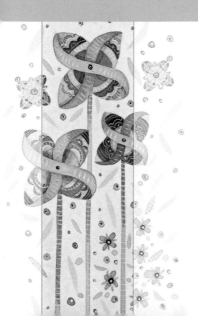

Life is never dull
with a daughter.

Little girls grow up when
you're not looking.

Small threads bind parents
and daughters together in love
and understanding.

September 13

Parents droop a little sometimes – but then
they think of their daughters – their verve and their
good-heartedness, their achievements and their beauty.
And feel much better.

April 22

Daughters grow, change
and weave most unexpected lives.
But still the wonder grows
– for in the alteration love persists.

September 12

Even the best of parents know
They are not owed anything.
They are paid
by all you give the world.

April 23

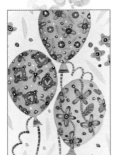

You have brought a sparkle
to my life.

September 11

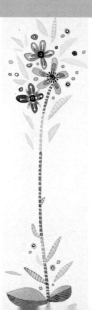

She doesn't love you any more, she says.
She scowls and turns away.
But, moments later, here she is against
your knee, her little arms about you,
her sweet, soft face nuzzling your rib cage.
A muffled, "Love you".
And the sun has come out again.

April 24

Thank you for giving me back stars
and fallen leaves,
winter beaches, summer woods.

September 10

Dear daughter,
sometimes,
things will go wrong.
The secret is
not to let them
overwhelm you.
Courage and hope
will see
you through.

Dearest daughter – we were
wonder-struck when we first saw your face,
first held your tiny hands.
We did not know that moment was only
the beginning of wonders.

A daughter can go
through a ballet class
like a sylph, like a swan,
change into dungarees
and head off
for a game of tennis
with the boys.

You have given my life
a greater meaning.

A lovely daughter, reflecting beauty
back into the world.
Making all things new.

When no one
can get through to anyone
by phone or e-mail
there are daughters
in the house.

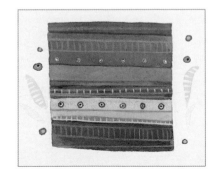

Daughters are an excuse for us
to indulge in the purchase
of quantities of little pink and frilly
garments and tiny, tiny shoes.

It's nice to have a daughter
to hand to plot parties.

September 6

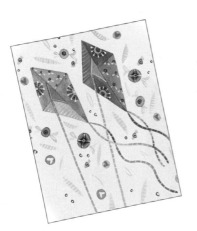

I suppose the best thing
I could wish you
would be enthusiasm.

Sometimes you just need someone to quietly hold you – and daughters know when.

September 5

Reach out to us and we are there.
As you have always been for us.

How can life ever be lonely
while we share the planet?

September 4

Mothers watch their daughters
toss themselves out of aircraft,
or vanish into the depths of the sea,
with a certain anxiety – but as they land,
or emerge from the waves like happy seals
– they rejoice. They could, by a trick of time,
been born Victorians.

Dear girl, I wish
that I could take your troubles
and bury them so deep
that they could never surface.
I can't.
But I am always here
to share them and help
as best I can
to set things right.

September 3

Who brings me small surprises?
Who makes me cups of tea? Who lets me watch
my programme though she's dying to change channels?
You my dearest daughter.
A daughter in a million.

Child. Clear crystal.
Bright and clear.
Faceted as none before you.
Catching the light from every
lovely thing and turning it
to rainbow.

September 2

A child gives us
our own first times,
all over again.

Thank you for sharing things with me.
Bars of chocolate. Cupcakes. Secrets.

September 1

I wish you what I have wished you since your life began:
May you never cease to search and challenge.
May you discover what you want to do – and do it well.

How very small you were.
The things I wished for you seemed too large
and ponderous for such a little creature.
So I gave you my finger to hold and a kiss
to welcome you into the world.

August 31

Here's my daughter,
the budding ballerina.
In a pink tutu.
On roller-skates.

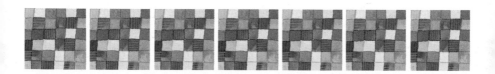

May 5

You are now utterly
independent and yet
I still share your joys
and your successes
and your sorrows.

August 30

Never forget – you're not just special to me.
You're special. And that's that.

Until you have a daughter
you don't realise how dull
your life has been.

August 29

Dearest Daughter – once I held you
in my arms. Now you are grown and free.
But I still hold you in my heart.

Mothers are proud of their grown-up daughters – but still hoard every memento of their childhood.

Some daughters give florists'
bouquets, Cartier watches
and Cointreau. Some daughters
send shrubs, sweaters
and home-made jam.
The thing is – daughters
know exactly what one needs.

All disappointments,
all failures fade like mist
before this golden girl.
Our daughter.

Daughters are given to making announcements. I've signed on to crew a boat to Singapore. I've invited my head teacher to dinner... Today. I'm leaving home. I'm going to be a nun. I'm having my hair dyed pink.

A small daughter's
life is beset with the need
to possess, to them,
most necessary gear.
Flat shoes and block shoes,
deck shoes and trainers.
A recorder and oboe.
A guitar. A bike.

August 26

You are my greatest treasure
– my dearest girl.

May 10

Like all past parents,
I send you on your way,
confident in all you
are and all you will become.
This is *your* time.
Delight in all it brings.
Things beyond imagination.

August 25

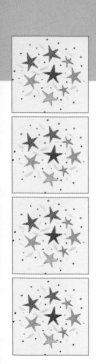

Dear Girl.
You changed my life.
Where I would be
without you I just don't know.
Not here.
Not as happy as I am.

Thank you for the years of wonder
that made you what you are.

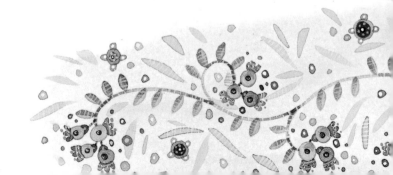

My most precious gift
– my dear lass.

Dear Daughter. Life has given you great power.
The ancients knew it. Your strength
outlasts all tyrannies,
all loss and sorrow, all changes and all bigotries.
You weave the world.
You know the heart of things.

August 23

You were my new beginning.

May 13

A daughter is a book
with a surprise on every page.

August 22

If I could, I would spare you all
the heart-sinking moments when
Happiness Goes Wrong.

Small daughters give their mothers
appalling gifts – plaster and plastic, glitter and shine.
Strange pots and stranger jewellery.
And their mothers give them a pride of place
and cherish them forever.

August 21

Every mother has drawers and boxes
overflowing with everything her children ever wrote
or drew or painted, stitched or made in woodwork.
The passing years held
like flies in amber.

Daughters are difficult.
Not every daughter perhaps.
There may be some who have never flounced
or stamped or pouted in their lives,
never flung themselves flat
or slammed doors hard behind them
in their later life. There may be...

Your daughter takes the paths
you never found.

May 16

All parents have to learn to take messages
and notes with equanimity... Bangkok.
Been in local hospital but OK now.
May go North at the end of the week.
Not sure where to, but will let you know soon.
P.S. Love to all!

You think she'll be a rosebud
– but be prepared
For a sunflower, an orchid or a daisy!
Daughters are wonderful.
But rarely what you expected.

You came – and my life
was changed forever.

With a daughter, life can never, never, never be monotonous.

They are all kept safe,
the birthday cards and Mother's Day cards
and little gifts, just because you thought
I'd like them. Tokens I have treasured
since you were small.
Amulets that heal my heart.

August 17

We hold each other's hearts in keeping.

May 19

Daughters come in every shape and size and disposition.
But you're the one for me.

The telephone is a wonderful thing.
It can offer a loving daughter a long distance
shoulder to cry on.

Daughters
spring surprises –
it's part
of their nature.

August 15

Every scrap of advice, every opinion,
every suggestion, every piece of useful information
that one gives a daughter vanishes like water
into sand. Until, long after, a grown-up daughter
gives her considered opinions upon some issue.
And one recognizes it.
Word for word.

My dearest girl,
you were a lovely baby,
a fascinating child
but look at you now!
A marvel!

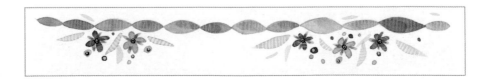

August 14

We field her as she falls.
Wrap her against the cold.
Boast casually to friends of her
achievements. Hoard photographs
in case we should forget.

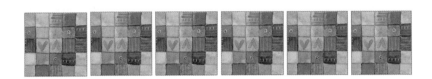

Did I ever tell you how proud I am of you,
or what delight you've given me?
No?
Then know it now.
Hold it in your heart.

August 13

You called today
and the sun came out.

May 23

Dear Daughter,
hold in your heart the joys
and sorrows of your childhood,
so that you can understand
those of your children.

August 12

No job, no man, no opportunity is ever quite good enough for one's daughter.

Dear Daughter,
May you do something
that you are proud of
– even if it is very small.

No mother's hands ever forget
her daughter's little bony hand
clasped safe in hers
on windy summer walks.

Thank you for turning up
when life had become monotonous.

From now on it is your journey.
Good luck.
Ride bravely. Ride well.

Dearest Daughter,
Thank you for being
exactly what you are.

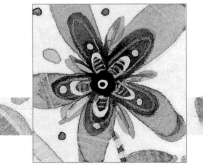

Grow, my dearest daughter,
learn and love. Skills you have never
yet suspected can be yours. Explore,
and find a place that's truly yours.

Having daughters
is the best investment
you will ever make against
becoming bored.

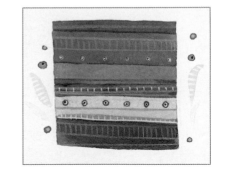

I sleep more soundly
when I know you're safe
and well and happy.

Daughters like to astonish their parents
– by showing abilities they never suspected.
A gift for mathematics. Cooking. Gardening.
Or flying aeroplanes. Perfect pitch. Or surgery.

When you were born,
you were an amazement
a perfection, a wonder.

In you I am young again.

You are our bright star.
You light our lives.

I've watched you grow
– and my love
has grown with you.

August 5

You walked and talked
and we were enchanted.
But all the time
you were turning from our dream
into your own reality.

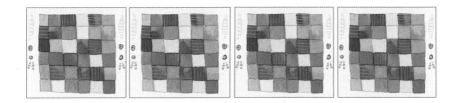

Thank you for making
every day a new adventure.

August 4

Daughters set out
on holiday to one
destination –
but e-mail you from
somewhere completely
different.
Generally remote and
a trifle dangerous.

As you grow older
I find more and more in you
to astonish and delight me.
How on earth did I manage
to produce such
a daughter?

So little time ago I took you to a café for a currant bun.
And now you are escorting me
into an astoundingly posh place for dinner.
But still my girl.

June 2

Your first mayfly. Your first rainbow.
Your first dinosaur.
Thank you for the chance to
rediscover the world.

August 2

Sometimes I wish I had treasures
to pass on to you.
But I gave what I could –
your five bright senses,
the world about you.

Daughters and Mothers
allow each other to fall off their respective diets
– just once in a while.

August 1

A wise parent never promises anything till they've checked the bank balance.

A daughter who travels
knows that she's fine.
And has no notion
that her mother and father
don't know that fact
and are out of their minds
with worry.

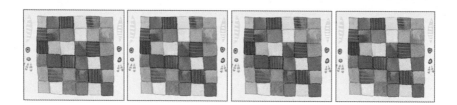

Thank you for making our lives
so incredibly eventful.

June 5

I have so many memories of you,
I have filed them away, wrapped in tissue,
tied with silver thread,
safe in the secret places of my mind.
So often, I take them out, fold back the papers,
hold them in my hand and smile.
I love you as you were and are and will be.

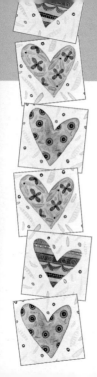

July 30

Parents may sigh to see their baby
grow into a schoolchild,
a schoolchild into an undergraduate,
an undergraduate into a professional
– with a life and loves all her own.
But they love her exactly the same.

With the birth of a daughter
one embarks on a lifetime's adventure.

I wish I could save you from
anxiety and sorrow…

We two most ordinary people
produced a marvel.
You opened your eyes,
looked at us and we knew
you were already
your own person –
and a small shiver of wonder
ran through us.

Now you bring me books and useful things
you pick up at the sales.
Best daughter in the world.

We have to let go their hands.
But the joys we knew before,
remembered,
are part of us all forever.

Some people seem to manage without a daughter.
They don't know what they're missing.

My beautiful, clever, warm-hearted daughter....
I try not to crow about you.
But I can't help looking a little smug.

I have other joys
– but the very best is you.

We showed you our world, but now you lead us into one we never knew.

You are our gift to the future.
With you the world is given
new opportunities, new vision.
In you lies hope.

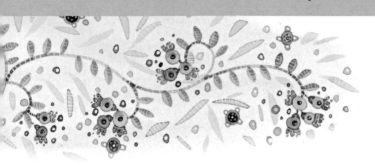

Her days are as precious as mine were.
They always will be.
Our children make their own wonders.

Dear, small, wide-eyed little daughter,
I'll hold your shadow in my arms forever,
even when you're grown.

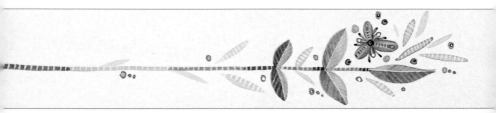

Mothers dream of daughters, before they come,
who will be academics, engineers, architects, artists,
dancers, doctors, operatic singers.
They get scruffs who climb trees.
Rodeo riders. Bank clerks. Train drivers.
And are absolutely delighted.

July 23

I will remember the first time I saw you
and hold it in my heart forever.

However important a daughter becomes,
however beautiful, however famous,
to her mother she is utterly unchanged.

July 22

A daughter is the person
you thought you would stop
worrying about when
she hits twenty-one.
But who is still
worrying you silly at forty-five.

Thank you for having given me the chance
to make mud pies again, to paddle in the sea,
to sail a toy boat – to ride the fairground horses.
Thank you for bringing back fun to all our lives.

July 21

Take courage, my lovely lass.
Whatever you do – do it well.
We are all behind you.

How can I call you mine
– when you belong to yourself
and to the world?
And yet, we are linked together
by love and memory
and so belong to one another.

I watched over you, fed you, protected you.
Be brave. Take possession of this sun bright air.

There is nothing, absolutely nothing
that can cheer up a dismal evening of TV repeats
and yesterday's leftovers more successfully
than a message from a daughter.

When I first saw you, you were charming.
But with every year you have grown until you are no longer
merely charming. You are magnificent. As a proud parent,
I think you're "Best in Show".

Do you remember spring walks?
Walking by a shining sea
and the sound of gulls? I do, I do.

A daughter is a member of
a self-perpetuating species.
Each only fully understands
why their mothers shrieked and tore
their hair out when their own
daughter hits the Teens.

There's one thing about daughters.
You're never sure who is going to step out
of the chaos they call their room.
An impeccably-groomed and dignified
young woman with her hair in a ballet knot,
a bright object with meticulously-ripped
jeans, a determined-looking girl in jodhpurs,
smelling faintly of horse
or a bleary-eyed student.

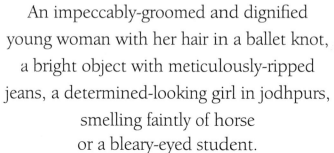

A daughter grows from a little loving child
into a dear companion.

I wish you discoveries and marvels.

July 16

Sometimes I come across a bit of paper
in your handwriting. A list.
A thank-you. And you're there in the room.
You always will be.

June 20

I am rediscovering
the world in you.
Seeing all things as if
for the first time.

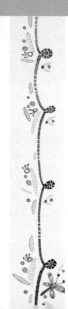

Every year makes you more dear.
Dear daughter –
What did I do to deserve you?

June 21

Daughters are so delightful one is tempted
to freeze-dry them when they are small – first teeth,
first steps, first words – unflawed forever.
But their glory is in their infinite capacity for change.

I watch you grow and change,
   a constant surprise,
   a constant wonder.

June 22

If I had the power to make one wish for you,
I would find it very hard to decide
what gift to give you –
what gift would help you to happiness.
But in the end, I am certain that
I would have chosen the best gift of all
– and that is courage.

A daughter's happiness
lights up a mother's heart – even if
that "child" is forty years old.

June 23

I wish I could take all your troubles
and wash them away,
hang out your days to blow in the sunshine.
Iron them and give them back to you
all fresh and sweet and good as new.

Daughters borrow things.
But give you their love in payment.

A parent lives
the suffering of a daughter –
made worse by her inability
to take it from her.

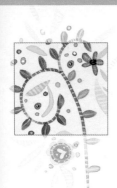

How could I manage without you?
Near or far from me
you give me hope and happiness.

It's good when a mother or father
and their daughter think of one another
– store things in their minds to tell each other.
People they've met, things they've done,
astonishments, delights.

Now you are moving on to new adventures, new loves, new friends but always, still, a part of us.

Daughters like you
are boxes of delight.

Dear Daughter
– explore the bits of the world I never got to,
read the books I never read.

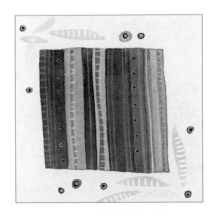

Daughters are
sugar and spice
– with a touch of Tabasco.

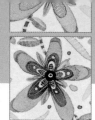

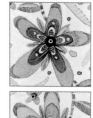

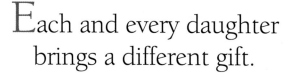

Each and every daughter
brings a different gift.

June 28

Thank you for every letter,
every note you've ever sent to me.
I have them all!

Thank you for giving me
the joys of childhood all over again.

Daughters are more precious
than one's dreams.

July 6

I saw such splendid things,
listened to such wonders,
And now your turn has come.
The world is waiting for you,
and the stars.

As long as you love me,
my dearest daughter,
I'm OK.

We were linked together by light, invisible chains – stronger than steel and indestructible.

July 1

A daughter often
has the courage
to do the things
you didn't dare.

Wave your daughter off
to university or Canada
and even as you dab your eyes
rejoice in her freedom
and courage.

Dearest Daughter.
Most puzzling, most exciting
and most loved.

How good it is,
to reach the café,
find a table, a cup of tea,
a quiet meal, a review of
the day's small triumphs.
My daughter
and my dearest friend.